SCHOLASTIC

READING

SATs CHALLENGE
YEAR 6

Skills Tests

FOR CHILDREN WORKING AT GREATER DEPTH

Book End, Range Road, Witney, Oxfordshire, OX29 0YD
Registered office: Westfield Road, Southam, Warwickshire CV47 0RA
www.scholastic.co.uk

© 2020, Scholastic Ltd

123456789   8901234567

British Library Cataloguing-in-Publication Data
A catalogue record for this book is available from the British Library.

ISBN 978-1407-18371-8
Printed and bound by Replika Press, India

All rights reserved. This book is sold subject to the condition that it shall not, by way of trade or otherwise, be lent, hired out or otherwise circulated without the publisher's prior consent in any form of binding or cover other than that in which it is published and without a similar condition, including this condition, being imposed upon the subsequent purchaser.

No part of this publication may be reproduced, stored in a retrieval system, or transmitted, in any form or by any means, electronic, mechanical, photocopying, recording or otherwise, other than for the purposes described in the content of this product, without the prior permission of the publisher. This product remains in copyright.

Every effort has been made to trace copyright holders for the works reproduced in this book, and the publishers apologise for any inadvertent omissions.

Author
Graham Fletcher

Editorial
Rachel Morgan, Shannon Keenlyside, Audrey Stokes, Suzanne Adams, Jennie Clifford and Sarah Chappelow

Series Design
Scholastic Design Team: Nicolle Thomas and Neil Salt

Layout
Dan Prescott/Couper Street Type Co

Cover Design
Scholastic Design Team: Nicolle Thomas and Neil Salt

Illustration
Adam Linley/Beehive Illustration

Contents

Advice for parents and carers 4

Advice for children 5

Progress chart 6

Reward certificate 7

1: *Oscar to the Rescue* (Fiction) 8

2: *Icarus and Daedelus* (Fiction) 16

3: *The Charge of the Light Brigade* (Poetry) 24

4: *Wheelchair Warrior* (Fiction) 30

5: *Skiathos* (Non-fiction) 38

6: *The Diary of Samuel Pepys* (Non-fiction) 45

7: *Hard Times* (Fiction) 52

8: *Brazil* (Non-fiction) 60

9: *Robinson Crusoe* (Fiction) 67

Answers 74

Answer grids 86

Reading

Advice for parents and carers

Children learn best when they do not feel under pressure and when they are free to explore ideas. Be flexible. If your child is distracted or tired they will not gain much from the practice.

This book allows children to apply what they have learned in key areas of the curriculum. The questions have been written to a higher level than usual and are meant to be challenging and to provide stretch. Supporting learning and understanding in this way will strengthen your child's grasp of key concepts. The questions can be used to assess areas to work on further. Follow up by offering opportunities to consolidate learning in a real-life setting and allow a break before working on further questions.

> Please note that if your child does not do well in answering these questions it is not an indication of poor performance in the National Tests. If you have any concerns, please discuss them with your child's teacher.

Use these tests however works best for you and your child but you may want to follow this approach:

- Take three of the tests from different genres to assess your child's knowledge and understanding (note there is only one poetry test). The questions for each text follow the same format with the focus clearly identified.
- Use the answer grids on pages 86–88 to identify in which areas your child needs more practice.
- Review these areas and practice skills in the related *Workbook (ISBN 978-1407-17555-3)*. Use the links in the answer grids to direct you to units you may wish to focus on or work through the *Workbook* unit by unit.
- Continue practising across all areas with three test texts and questions of your choice.
- Once you feel your child has had enough opportunity to build up their skills, take the remaining three tests and mark it to assess their progress. Review topics as necessary.

These practice tests contain more questions and answers than is usual for each text in the Key Stage 2 Reading National Test. There are also more high-tariff questions and fewer selected answers than in the National Tests.

Advice for children

Are you ready to take the challenge? The texts and questions in this book are tricky but they will help you to see how much you understand.

> Don't worry if you don't manage to answer every question or if you get some answers wrong. We learn from our mistakes.

- Find a quiet place to work.
- Have a positive mindset – focus on what you know. Remember that mistakes make our brain grows!
- Take your time – don't start the challenge if you are in a rush to do something else.
- Review your work.

These tests have been ordered by the subject area (for example, inference, prediction and so on). Therefore, they do not match the National Test format exactly and test skills, such as the questions being in order of the text or the more difficult questions coming last, will not necessarily be true here. These tests are to help you practice the types of question you will encounter in the tests, they are not 'mock' tests.

Reading

Progress chart

Test	Taken	Practised	Achieved
1: *Oscar to the Rescue* (Fiction)			
2: *Icarus and Daedelus* (Fiction)			
3: *The Charge of the Light Brigade* (Poetry)			
4: *Wheelchair Warrior* (Fiction)			
5: *Skiathos* (Non-fiction)			
6: *The Diary of Samuel Pepys* (Non-fiction)			
7: *Hard Times* (Fiction)			
8: *Brazil* (Non-fiction)			
9: *Robinson Crusoe* (Fiction)			

… SCHOLASTIC

Reward Certificate

Well done!

I've aimed higher with SATs Challenge

Name: _____ Date: _____

My strongest areas are:

_____

_____

I will challenge myself to fly higher in:

_____

1: *Oscar to the Rescue*

1: *Oscar to the Rescue*

Chapter One

Oscar opened the back door and waved goodbye to his mum.

"Whatever you do, make sure you're back in time for tea!" she called.

"Yes, Mum, I'm just taking the dog for a walk," he replied.

Closing the door quickly, he traversed the yard and opened the gate. He stood in the passageway and waited for **it** to happen.

He did not know when it would happen. He did not know how it would happen. He did not know why it would happen. He just knew that it **would** happen.

Oscar stood and waited, not knowing exactly what would take place, and then **it** happened.

The sky turned a menacing shade of black and a strong wind gusted down the passageway. Oscar realised that he was not alone. A tall man dressed in black loomed forebodingly over him and put his hand ominously on the boy's shoulder.

"Come this way. Quickly! There is not a moment to lose!"

Chapter Two

Oscar wasn't astonished or frightened. This was how **it** always happened. Whenever his mother said, "Whatever you do, make sure you're back in time for tea!" and Oscar went through the gate, something happened. The weather always changed and there was always someone waiting for him.

Today, it was the tall man in black. The sky transformed into a leaden grey and driving snow began to fall incessantly. Oscar found himself trudging through deeper and deeper snow. His Labrador dog, Kaiser, leaped and bounded along next to him, delighted to be out. To his right, Oscar saw a mountain that he recognised instantly.

"It's the Matterhorn!"

"Yes," said the tall man. "Thank goodness you're here. There has been a terrible landslide. Two children have been swept away in it. We can't find them. You are their only chance."

"Me?"

"Yes. You and the dog. Get on the train. It's the only way to get further up the mountain."

1: *Oscar to the Rescue*

Chapter Three

Oscar's dog sat next to him quietly. The train pulled in.

"Come on, Kaiser."

They left the comparative warmth and safety of the railway station and stood in the street outside, unsure which way to go. Kaiser raised her nose and sniffed the air, inhaling it deeply. Suddenly her snout pointed almost vertically upwards, twitching animatedly, as she stared into the distance.

"What do you think, Kaiser, shall we start over there?"

Kaiser got up and moved up the slope through the snow with substantial difficulty. Oscar followed in her tracks, the snow coming up to his waist. There were no signs of any footprints ahead and the snow was rapidly filling in their own, obliterating them. Oscar turned round to check the way back but all he could see was a pristine blanket of snow. More snow was falling heavily. Oscar could not see the buildings they had left such a short time ago. Suddenly the Matterhorn had gone too.

Within seconds they were completely lost!

Chapter Four

"Kaiser! Kaiser! Where are you, girl?"

Oscar could not see or hear Kaiser. The howling wind swirled round him, sweeping snow into his eyes and deafening his ears. Suddenly he felt very much alone. The man in black had not come with them when they left the railway station. Oscar looked around but could see nothing. The safety of the children depended on him and Kaiser, and now he had lost his faithful canine companion. What chance had he now? Oscar was very perturbed but he knew what he had to do. He did what he always did. He put his hand into his pocket knowing that **something** would be in there. He did not know what it would be but he knew that **it** would help him. It always happened that way.

Oscar reached deeply into his pocket. There **was** something there!

Slowly and delicately, Oscar extracted the object from his pocket. He knew immediately that it was a torch. He also knew that the torch was not the only thing in his pocket. He reached in

1: Oscar to the Rescue

again and pulled out a long silver tube. It was a whistle and Oscar knew that if he blew loudly enough on it, people would be able to hear him and come to his rescue. It would not help him find Kaiser but he would have to deal with that problem afterwards.

Oscar raised the whistle to his lips, took a huge breath and blew with all of his might. Nothing! Not a sound. Not a peep. He blew again on the whistle as hard as he could. His cheeks turned crimson and he could feel his blood pounding, drumming in his ears. Still nothing!

Oscar was perplexed. This had never happened before. Whenever he had faced dilemmas previously, all he had had to do was to reach into his pocket and there would be something that would help him. This useless piece of metal was no good. It wasn't doing anything. It wasn't getting him saved and it wasn't helping him find Kaiser.

He stood for a minute, convinced that he was destined to be doomed forever. He wasn't sure but, almost indiscernibly in the distance, he thought he could hear a dog barking. Suddenly he knew he was right. Kaiser came crashing through the snow and almost knocked him over, leaping up and licking his chin.

"Kaiser! Where have you been? How did you find me? Am I glad to see you!"

Kaiser licked the whistle in Oscar's hand passionately. Of course! A dog whistle! That was why Oscar couldn't hear it.

"Well, now you're back, we'd better get looking for these missing children."

Oscar looked around him. There were no clues about which way to go. He shone the torch in front of him but still there was nothing to be seen.

"Well, Kaiser, where do you think we should start? If we don't move soon we'll become snowmen. Well, I will – you'll be a snow dog."

Without knowing where he was going or why, Oscar set off walking as quickly as he could uphill with Kaiser scampering after him. If only he had an idea of where to go.

From Oscar to the Rescue by Graham Fletcher, 2017

1: *Oscar to the Rescue*

These questions are all about *Oscar to the Rescue* on pages 8–10.

Words in context

1. *There were no signs of any footprints ahead and the snow was rapidly filling in their own, **obliterating** them.*

    What does *obliterating* mean in this sentence?

    _____

    1

2. *He stood for a minute, convinced that he was **destined** to be doomed forever.*

    Circle the word that is closest in meaning to *destined*.

    | never | fated | soon | going |

    1

3. *He wasn't sure but, almost **indiscernibly** in the distance, he thought he could hear a dog barking.*

    Draw a line to join *indiscernibly* to its meaning in this sentence.

    indiscernibly

    loudly

    unnoticeably

    obviously

    invisibly

    1

1: *Oscar to the Rescue*

Retrieval/identification

4. From Chapter Two, **find** and **copy two** things that always take place when *it* happens.

1. _____

2. _____ **1**

5. What has caused the two children to be lost?

_____ **1**

6. Give **two** things that Oscar finds in his pocket.

1. _____

2. _____ **1**

Summarising main ideas

7. Give **three** ways Oscar is seen as a hero throughout the extract.

1. _____
_____

2. _____
_____

3. _____
_____ **3**

1: *Oscar to the Rescue*

Inference

Marks

8. *A tall man dressed in black loomed forebodingly over him and put his hand ominously on the boy's shoulder.*

Give **three** words from the sentence above that suggest that Oscar could be in danger.

1. _____

2. _____

3. _____

1

9. From Chapter Two, why wasn't Oscar surprised or frightened?

_____

_____

1

10. From Chapter Three, give **two** reasons why Kaiser might have *moved up the slope through the snow with substantial difficulty?*

1. _____

2. _____

2

1: Oscar to the Rescue

Inference

11. From Chapter Four, give **two** reasons why there might not have been any clues about which way to go.

1. _____

2. _____

Marks: 2

12. From Chapter Four, give **two** reasons why Oscar might have felt *very much alone*.

1. _____

2. _____

Marks: 2

Prediction

13. What is likely to happen to Oscar, Kaiser and the lost children? Give a reason for your answer.

_____

_____

Marks: 2

1: *Oscar to the Rescue*

Marks

How information is related

14. How does the ending of each chapter make you want to read on?

_____

_____

1

How meaning is enhanced

15. In Chapter one, the words *it* and *would* are emphasised. What effect does this have on the reader?

_____

_____

2

Making comparisons

16. How is Oscar different at the beginning and end of the extract?

_____

_____

2

End of test

2: Icarus and Daedalus

Daedalus lived hundreds of years ago. He was a skilful artist who used his considerable talent to design buildings and temples. He was probably the finest architect of his time.

In Crete there lived a powerful king – Minos. You will almost certainly have heard of him. His favourite pet was a malicious monster called the Minotaur. It had the head of a bull and the body of a man. It lived by eating human sacrifices. Minos asked Daedalus to design a place for the monster to live. It was to be a perplexing underground maze called the Labyrinth.

Daedalus did not approve of the monster but he had to earn money so he took the job. He did not dare tell Minos what he thought. It was a difficult job because the Labyrinth had to keep both the people of Crete and the Minotaur safe. It had to be so complicated that no one would be able to find their way in to get to the monster and the monster would not be able to find its way out to attack the people.

Daedalus had a son, Icarus, who he brought to the island with him. When the Labyrinth was completed, Minos was very pleased with it. Icarus and Daedalus stayed on the island as his honoured guests. This happy time was destroyed when Theseus came to Crete and killed the Minotaur. Minos suspected that Daedalus had helped him. As far as Minos was concerned, that was the only solution. No one else could possibly have found their way through the intricate tunnel system. How else would Theseus have been able to get into and out of the Labyrinth safely? Daedalus and Icarus were no longer guests. They were prisoners.

Daedalus could not prove his innocence and feared further punishment. He expected to be tortured mercilessly. He needed to find a way to escape from the island but they could not get to the port to find a boat. While he was thinking of ways to escape, Daedalus enviously watched the birds that flew freely above him. That was the answer. Wings! If they could not sail away, they could fly.

Surreptitiously, so as not to arouse suspicion, Daedalus and Icarus began collecting bird feathers. Bit by bit, Daedalus carefully glued the delicate feathers together with wax until he had two complete pairs of wings. They were ready for their flight.

2: Icarus and Daedalus

With the wings firmly attached to their arms, the pair of them flapped furiously. Slowly at first, then more quickly, they began to rise up. They were flying! Daedalus warned Icarus not to fly too high as the sun was dangerous. Soon Crete was a distant memory. They sped above the clear blue ocean, with their troubles all behind them. They couldn't have been happier.

Icarus loved it all. He was a very confident flyer.

"Look at me!" he cried. "See how high I can fly!"

He flew higher and higher, soaring above Daedalus, who shouted to him, warning him again about the sun. Icarus flew so high and so fast that he was soon out of earshot. No matter what his father shouted, Icarus could not hear it. Would he have listened if he could? Probably not. He was enjoying himself so much that he didn't really care.

Gradually, the heat of the sun began to melt the wax on Icarus' wings. It was imperceptible at first. By the time Icarus felt the hot wax on his arms, it was too late. The flimsy wings fell apart and dropped into the water. Icarus tried to flap his arms faster but without the wings it was no use. He followed them rapidly into the sea.

Daedalus watched from above. He circled the spot where Icarus had disappeared but he did not return to the surface. Daedalus swooped downwards, skimming the waves, risking his own life to search for his son, but it was no use. Icarus did not reappear.

Daedalus, filled with guilt and regret, had little choice but to continue alone. Too afraid to look back, he slowly flew away, wishing that he had never designed anything in his life.

2: Icarus and Daedalus

These questions are all about *Icarus and Daedalus* on pages 16 and 17.

Words in context

1. *His favourite pet was a **malicious** monster called the Minotaur.*

    Tick the word or phrase that is closest in meaning to *malicious* in this sentence.

    Tick one.

    | harmless | ☐ | inoffensive | ☐ |
    | wicked | ☐ | hungry | ☐ |

    1

2. **Surreptitiously**, *so as not to arouse suspicion*

    What does *Surreptitiously* mean in this sentence?

    _____

    1

3. *The **flimsy** wings fell apart*

    Draw a line to join *flimsy* to its meaning in this sentence.

    flimsy

    sturdy

    strong

    fragile

    wide

    1

2: *Icarus and Daedalus*

Retrieval/identification

4. What did Daedalus use his *considerable talent* to design?

_____

5. Give **one** reason why Icarus could not hear Daedalus shouting to warn him about the sun.

_____

6. Put a tick in the correct box to show whether each of the following statements is **true** or **false**.

	True	False
Daedalus was definitely the finest architect of his time.		
You will certainly have heard of Minos.		
Daedalus' wings were made from feathers and wax.		
Daedalus tried to warn Icarus about the sun.		

Marks

1

1

1

2: *Icarus and Daedalus*

Summarising main ideas

Marks

7. Give **three** occasions when Daedalus was scared in the extract.

1. _____
2. _____
3. _____

3

Inference

8. Give **one** reason why Daedalus might not have approved of the Minotaur.

_____
_____

1

9. Give **two** reasons why Minos might have suspected Daedalus of helping Theseus.

1. _____
2. _____

2

2: Icarus and Daedalus

Inference

Marks

10. Give **one** reason why Minos might have wanted to keep Daedalus and Icarus on the island as *honoured guests*.

_____

1

11. Give **two** reasons why Daedalus could not prove his innocence.

1. _____

_____

2. _____

_____

2

12. Give **three** reasons why Daedalus might have felt *filled with guilt and regret* at the end of the extract.

1. _____
2. _____
3. _____

3

2: *Icarus and Daedalus*

Inference

13. Give **two** reasons why Daedalus might have felt he had *little choice but to continue alone.*

1. _____

2. _____

Marks

2

Prediction

14. Give **one** thing Minos might do when he finds that Daedalus and Icarus have escaped.

_____

_____

1

How information is related

15. Give **two** ways that the final sentence links to the rest of the extract.

1. _____

_____

2. _____

_____

2

2: *Icarus and Daedalus*

How meaning is enhanced

16. Look at the paragraph beginning *Daedalus could not prove his innocence and feared further punishment.*

Find and **copy one** phrase that shows how terrible he thought his punishment would be.

_____

1

Making comparisons

17. How does Minos' attitude towards Daedalus change during the extract?

_____

_____

_____

2

End of test

3: The Charge of the Light Brigade

1. Half a league, half a league,
   Half a league onward,
   All in the valley of Death
   Rode the six hundred.
   "Forward, the Light Brigade!
   Charge for the guns!" he said:
   Into the valley of Death
   Rode the six hundred.

2. "Forward, the Light Brigade!"
   Was there a man dismayed?
   Not though the soldier knew
   Someone had blundered:
   Theirs not to make reply,
   Theirs not to reason why,
   Theirs but to do and die:
   Into the valley of Death
   Rode the six hundred.

3. Cannon to right of them,
   Cannon to left of them,
   Cannon in front of them
   Volleyed and thundered;
   Stormed at with shot and shell,
   Boldly they rode and well,
   Into the jaws of Death,
   Into the mouth of Hell
   Rode the six hundred.

4. Flashed all their sabres bare,
   Flashed as they turned in air
   Sabring the gunners there,
   Charging an army, while
   All the world wondered:
   Plunged in the battery-smoke
   Right through the line they broke;
   Cossack and Russian
   Reeled from the sabre-stroke
   Shattered and sundered.
   Then they rode back, but not
   Not the six hundred.

5. Cannon to right of them,
   Cannon to left of them,
   Cannon behind them
   Volleyed and thundered;
   Stormed at with shot and shell,
   While horse and hero fell,
   They that had fought so well
   Came through the jaws of Death
   Back from the mouth of Hell,
   All that was left of them,
   Left of six hundred.

6. When can their glory fade?
   O the wild charge they made!
   All the world wondered.
   Honour the charge they made,
   Honour the Light Brigade,
   Noble six hundred.

Alfred Lord Tennyson

3: The Charge of the Light Brigade

These questions are all about 'The Charge of the Light Brigade' on page 24.

Marks

Words in context

1. *Someone had* **blundered**:

   What does *blundered* mean in this sentence?

   _____

   1

2. **Honour** *the Light Brigade,*

   Circle **one** word that is closest in meaning to *Honour*.

   reward   refuse   replace   respect

   1

3. **Noble** *six hundred!*

   Draw a line to join *Noble* to its meaning in this sentence.

   noble   fair

   generous

   sporting

   splendid

   1

3: *The Charge of the Light Brigade*

Retrieval/identification

Marks

4. From Verse 1, what were the men ordered to attack?

_____

1

5. Give **three** places where the cannons were.

1. _____
2. _____
3. _____

1

6. From Verse 4, **find** and **copy** the names of **two** groups of people that the soldiers were attacking.

1. _____
2. _____

1

Summarising main ideas

7. Number the events below to show the order in which they happen in the poem. The first one has been done for you.

The Light Brigade is ordered to attack.	1
The soldiers use their sabres.	☐
The Light Brigade ride back from the mouth of Hell.	☐
The soldiers do not question their order.	☐
The Light Brigade ride into the jaws of Death.	☐

1

3: *The Charge of the Light Brigade*

Inference

Marks

8. **Find** and **copy three** phrases that explain why the soldiers did not question their orders.

   1. _____
   2. _____
   3. _____

   1

9. *the jaws of Death*

   Give **three** things this tells us about the battlefield.

   1. _____
   2. _____
   3. _____

   3

10. From Verse 4, give **one** reason why *All the world wondered.*

    _____
    _____

    1

11. From Verse 5, **find** and **copy** the word that tells us the poet thought the men died gloriously.

    _____

    1

3: *The Charge of the Light Brigade*

Inference

12. From Verse 5, **find** and **copy** a phrase that shows that the Light Brigade suffered heavy losses.

    _____

    Marks

    1

13. In the last verse, what impression is the poet trying to give of the Light Brigade?

    _____

    1

Prediction

14. What are readers of the poem likely to think about the Charge?

    _____
    _____

    1

How information is related

15. How does the poet emphasise the number of soldiers in the Light Brigade?

    _____

    1

3: *The Charge of the Light Brigade*

How meaning is enhanced

16. *Stormed at with shot and shell* (Verse 3)

What does this tell you about the ammunition that was fired at the Light Brigade?

_____

_____

2

Making comparisons

17. Read Verse 3 and Verse 5. How has the position of the cannons changed?

_____

_____

2

End of test

4: Wheelchair Warrior

Elliott Walsh has been involved in a motorcycle accident. At this point in the story, he is in a coma in hospital.

Elliott was awake but he could not see. Perhaps it was still dark. He could not move either. Perhaps he was just exhausted. He could hear people talking. They were near to him. Where was he? What was he doing there? What were they doing there? He tried to call out but they did not seem to hear him.

The voices were hushed, almost strained, but Elliott could just, only just, make out what they were saying.

"So what are you saying, Doctor?"

It was his mother's voice. Again the question came back, where was he? Now there were other questions. She was talking to a doctor. Why?

"It's too early to say, Mrs Walsh."

"What does that mean?"

Her voice was low and quiet, fearing the worst but hoping for the best. Somehow Elliott, as if eavesdropping, listened to the reply with her, echoing her feelings.

"There's no easy way to say this, Mrs Walsh."

There was a slight pause as the doctor fumbled to find the softest words. Failing completely, he opted for the simplest, most brutal method. Get it over with quickly. Cut it away as he would a cancer in the operating theatre.

"He might never walk again."

Elliott's mother did not reply but Elliott could hear her sobbing softly. Why? Who was the 'He' the doctor was talking about?

Suddenly, it hit Elliott with the force of a hurricane. The full ferocity of it lashed him across the face as he realised that he was the "He". Bewilderment strangled his senses as he tried to comprehend what he had heard. "He might never walk again." Those were the words. Why?

He began to realise why he could not move. He was paralysed. Held in the grip of suspended animation by a cruel, invisible captor. How? He could not think of a reason. How had this happened? He searched his memory as carefully as a bomb disposal expert would a lethal minefield, trying to bring its terrifying contents to the surface.

At first there was nothing. Then, slowly, one shred began to emerge. Gradually, he prised it from its hiding place. The last thing he could remember was the race, the final one of the season. He didn't even need to win the race to claim the British Junior Championship. Anything in the top four and he would have done it. It had been easy. No one could stay with him that day. He remembered coming up the last slope and reaching the top of the hill. He remembered

4: Wheelchair Warrior

the bike taking off as he rode the jump. He remembered the sunlight glaring across his visor. Then, he remembered nothing. Just blackness. Nothing there.

"We'll keep him in intensive care. He's connected to the monitors. We'll know if anything changes. It's really a case now of wait and see. Try talking to him. Although he is in a coma, I'm sure he can hear you. He will be aware you are there."

Elliott's mother came closer to him. He could sense her presence but that was all. When she held his hand he was aware of something warm but above that he could feel nothing. He felt like his head had become a prison from which there was no escape into the rest of his body.

His mother's voice was speaking. The words didn't make much sense but he heard them just the same.

"We'll be waiting for you when you get through all this, Elliott. Your dad and I will be there for you."

He heard the door swish as the doctor opened it. He heard his mother's heels as they clicked across the floor, gradually moving away from him. He heard them slow down as she reached the door.

"Mum, I'm here!" he screamed. "Why are you leaving?" His brain roared the words but no sound left his lips. He pleaded with her to stay, not to go and leave him alone with the machines and the monitors. As the voice in his head threatened to deafen him, Elliott was convinced his mother must be able to hear him.

Elliott's mother turned back towards her son. His voice thundered around the emptiness of his head. He had screamed so loudly that his mother must have heard him. At first he thought she had and was coming back, but she was only taking one last look. Abruptly, she pulled a tissue from her pocket, dabbed it at her eyes and turned quickly to leave, sobbing quietly.

He watched her leave through glistening eyes that showed nothing. Why was it that he bled emotion inside his body? Was no one sensitive enough to staunch the flow or stem the haemorrhage?

**From Wheelchair Warrior
by Graham Fletcher, 2017**

4: Wheelchair Warrior

These questions are all about *Wheelchair Warrior* on pages 30 and 31.

Words in context

1. **Bewilderment** *strangled his senses as he tried to comprehend what he had heard.*

   What does *Bewilderment* mean in this sentence?

   _____

   Marks: 1

2. *He remembered the sunlight glaring across his* **visor**.

   Circle **one** word that is closest in meaning to *visor*.

   | eyebrow | eyeshade | eyeball | eyesight |

   Marks: 1

3. *Was no one sensitive enough to* **staunch** *the flow or stem the haemorrhage?*

   Draw a line to join *staunch* to its meaning in this sentence.

   staunch

   loyal
   stop
   help
   increase

   Marks: 1

4: Wheelchair Warrior

Retrieval/identification

Marks

4. From the paragraph beginning *He began to realise why he could not move*, **find** and **copy** the phrase that tells us how Elliott searched his memory.

_____

_____

1

5. From the paragraph beginning *At first there was nothing*, **find** and **copy three** things that Elliott remembers from immediately before the crash.

1. _____

2. _____

3. _____

2

6. Give **three** sounds Elliott hears as his mother leaves.

1. _____

2. _____

3. _____

1

4: Wheelchair Warrior

Summarising main ideas

7. Give **three** things the doctor tells Elliott's mother about Elliott's condition.

1. _____
2. _____
3. _____

Marks

2

Inference

8. *The voices were hushed, almost strained, but Elliott could just, only just, make out what they were saying.*

Give **one** reason why the doctor and Elliott's mother might have been talking quietly.

_____

_____

1

9. Read the paragraph beginning *At first there was nothing.* Give **two** reasons why Elliott might not have been able to remember what happened.

1. _____
2. _____

2

4: *Wheelchair Warrior*

Inference

Marks

10. Give **two** reasons why the doctor might have found it difficult to explain what had happened to Elliott's mother.

1. _____

2. _____

2

11. Give **three** reasons why the doctor might have chosen to explain about Elliott being paralysed using *the simplest, most brutal method*.

1. _____

2. _____

3. _____

3

12. From the paragraph beginning *"We'll keep him in intensive care"*, give **one** way the doctors will know if Elliott's condition changes.

_____

1

4: Wheelchair Warrior

Inference

13. *"We'll be waiting for you when you get through all this, Elliott. Your dad and I will be there for you."*

    Why might his mother's words not have made much sense to Elliott?

    _____

    _____

    1

Prediction

14. What is likely to happen to Elliott next?

    _____

    _____

    _____

    1

How information is related

15. Give **three** occasions when Elliott does not understand what is happening.

    1. _____

    _____

    2. _____

    _____

    3. _____

    _____

    3

4: Wheelchair Warrior

How meaning is enhanced

16. *He felt like his head had become a prison from which there was no escape into the rest of his body.*

Give **two** ways that Elliott's head has become *a prison*.

1. _____

2. _____

2

17. *Gradually, he prised it from its hiding place.*

What does this tell us about how hard Elliott found it to remember what had happened to him?

_____
_____
_____

2

Making comparisons

18. How does Elliott change during the extract?

_____
_____
_____

2

End of test

5: Skiathos

This article is about the Greek island, Skiathos.

The island

Skiathos is not the largest of the Sporades islands but it is the most important. Its airport is a gateway to the other major islands of Skopelos and Alonissos. Ferries and fast catamarans link the islands in a daily service that criss-crosses the short distance between them.

Most visitors don't get past Skiathos. Some don't even get past Skiathos town, a short distance from the airport. I have been there many times and I have always been enchanted by it. I fell in love with the island on my first visit. Our tour rep said that Skiathos was known as the 'boomerang island'. Having returned so many times, I understand completely what he meant.

My first time in the Sporades was spent entirely on Skiathos. Future trips saw me visit Skopelos then Alonissos. Most recently I have been island-hopping to all three. Those who stay in Skiathos will have a wonderful time but they will not experience the difference and charms of the less visited, more relaxed and quieter islands.

Spend a day in Skiathos town and you'll be able to lose yourself in a labyrinth of cobbled streets, bars and tiny shops. To find your way out, just remember, it's downhill to the harbour. That's if you want to find your way out, of course.

The beaches

The island is less than nine miles long and four miles wide, yet it packs in over 60 fabulous beaches. At the far west of the island is the massive Koukounaries beach, a resort aimed at attracting families and young people with water sports and music. The smaller resorts of Troulos and Agia Paraskevi are aimed at a different clientele. Whatever your taste, you'll always find a tavern or two selling cold, refreshing drinks and authentic Greek food. Believe me, in the heat of the midday sun, you'll appreciate the shade they offer.

If you want real peace and solitude, head for the northern beaches. They aren't easily accessible. You'll need hire transport that can cover sandy tracks through pine forests or you'll have to walk. I walked. Most people find it too difficult. I was very warm by the time I got there but it was worth the effort. A taverna, a glorious sea view and an almost empty beach. That's heaven for me.

5: *Skiathos*

Transport

You can hire a car or a motorbike but my advice is: don't bother. The island is so small that it's not worth it. Besides, the bus service is so good that you'll find you don't need your own transport, unless you really want to go off-road. There is a bus service along the island's main road every 20 minutes, but it is not so frequent in winter. It will carry you all the way from Koukounaries to Skiathos town for about two euros. The places in between aren't known by their names. They are called by the bus stop numbers! If you get off at Bus Stop 12 at Tzaneria, you'll find there is also a water taxi to Skiathos that returns late at night.

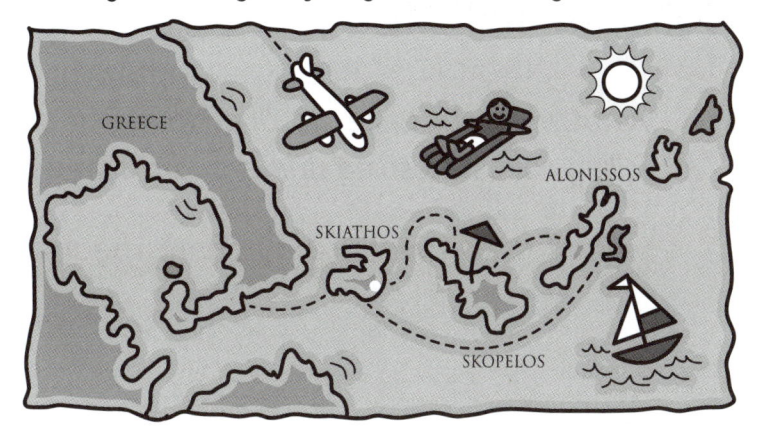

Skiathos Airport

I can't finish without mentioning the airport. If you've been, you'll know why. You come in low over the harbour and land on a very short runway. At the end of it there is a small beach and the sea! It's a great place to watch the planes take off as they fly right over you. In the airport terminal, you'll see lots of pictures of planes flying low over the town to land. It can't be that dangerous though, as there aren't any pictures of crashes!

A top tip when you're leaving Skiathos is to go to the airport, check in and drop your bags off. That's normal. What's not normal is then to leave the airport and go to the taverna across the road. Most people go straight into Departures but it's very small and cramped. Why squash yourself in with all the sun-loving lobsters when you can relax in a spacious garden? You won't miss your plane because you'll be able to watch it land in front of you.

When you come back

It's not *if* you come back, it's *when*. Don't just stay on Skiathos. You'll be richly rewarded for taking the short trips to Skopelos and Alonissos. They both have a flavour of Skiathos but they are also distinctly unique. I love the harbour-front cafes on both of them. To tell you more would be to spoil it for you. Don't take my word for it. Go find out for yourself, but be warned: you won't be able to resist the boomerang.

5: *Skiathos*

These questions are all about *Skiathos* on pages 38 and 39.

Words in context

1. *Whatever your taste, you'll always find a tavern or two, selling cold, refreshing drinks and* **authentic** *Greek food.*

   What does the word *authentic* mean in this sentence?

   _____

   Marks: 1

2. *The smaller resorts of Troulos and Agia Paraskevi are aimed at a different* **clientele**.

   Circle **one** word that is closest in meaning to *clientele*.

   | tourists | customers | targets | hotels |

   Marks: 1

3. *They both have a flavour of Skiathos but they are also distinctly* **unique**.

   Draw a line to join *unique* to its meaning in this sentence.

   unique

   original
   common
   similar
   ordinary

   Marks: 1

5: *Skiathos*

Retrieval/identification

Marks

4. Give **two** ways to travel between the Sporades islands.

1. _____

2. _____

1

5. From the section 'Transport', **find** and **copy two** reasons why it is not worth hiring a car.

1. _____

_____

2. _____

_____

1

6. From the section 'Skiathos Airport', give **two** things that are **not** normal.

1. _____

2. _____

2

5: *Skiathos*

Summarising main ideas

7. Using information from the text, tick one box in each row to show whether each statement is **true** or **false**.

	True	False
Skiathos is an island in the Sporades.		
The beaches of Troulos and Agia Paraskevi are aimed at young people.		
The bus will take you from Koukounaries to Skiathos town for about two euros.		
Planes fly low over the town to land at the airport.		

Marks

1

Inference

8. Read the paragraph beginning *Spend a day in Skiathos town*. Suggest **one** reason why you might not want to find your way out.

_____

_____

1

9. Give **two** reasons why the beaches on the northern coast are almost empty.

1. _____

2. _____

2

Inference

10. Give **one** reason why the bus service is likely to be less frequent in the winter.

_____

Marks

1

11. Give **two** reasons why the airport terminal might not have any pictures of crashes.

1. _____

2. _____

2

12. From the final paragraph, give **one** reason why *To tell you more would be to spoil it for you.*

_____

1

13. Give **one** reason why you will not be able to *resist the boomerang*.

_____

1

Prediction

14. Give **two** things that are likely to happen to people who have been to Skiathos.

1. _____

2. _____

2

5: *Skiathos*

Marks

How information is related

15. Give **three** ways that the final paragraph links to the section headed 'The island'.

1. _____

2. _____

3. _____

3

How meaning is enhanced

16. *Why squash yourself in with all the sun-loving lobsters...?*

Give **two** reasons why the writer describes the tourists as *sun-loving lobsters*.

1. _____

2. _____

2

Making comparisons

17. Give **three** ways that Skopelos and Alonissos are different to Skiathos.

1. _____

2. _____

3. _____

3

End of test

6: The Diary of Samuel Pepys

2nd September 1666

Jane called us up about three in the morning, to tell us of a great fire they saw in the City. So I rose and slipped on my nightgown, and went to her window, and thought it to be on the backside of Mark Lane at the farthest; but, being unused to such fires as followed, I thought it far enough off; and so went to bed again and to sleep.

About seven rose again to dress myself, and there looked out at the window, and saw the fire not so much as it was and further off. By and by Jane comes and tells me that she hears that above 300 houses have been burned down tonight by the fire we saw, and that it is now burning down all Fish Street, by London Bridge.

So I made myself ready presently, and walked to the Tower, and there got up upon one of the high places and there I did see the houses at that end of the bridge all on fire, and an infinite great fire on this and the other side the end of the bridge; which, among other people, did trouble me for poor little Michell and our Sarah on the bridge.

So down, with my heart full of trouble, to the Lieutenant of the Tower, who tells me that it began this morning in the King's baker's house in Pudding Lane, and that it hath burned St. Magnus' Church and most part of Fish Street already. So I down to the water side, and there got a boat and through bridge, and there saw a lamentable fire. Poor Michell's house, as far as the Old Swan, already burned that way, and the fire running further, that in a very little time it got as far as the Steelyard, while I was there. Everybody endeavouring to remove their goods, and flinging into the river or bringing them into lighters that lay off; poor people staying in their houses as long as till the very fire touched them, and then running into boats, or clambering from one pair of stairs by the water-side to another.

6: The Diary of Samuel Pepys

Having stayed, and in an hour's time seen the fire rage every way, and nobody, to my sight, endeavouring to quench it, but to remove their goods, and leave all to the fire, and having seen it get as far as the Steelyard, and the wind mighty high and driving it into the City; I to Whitehall and there up to the King's closet in the Chapel, where people come about me, and did give them an account dismayed them all, and word was carried in to the King. So I was called for and did tell the King and Duke of York what I saw, and that unless his Majesty did command houses to be pulled down nothing could stop the fire. They seemed much troubled, and the King commanded me to go to my Lord Mayor and command him to spare no houses, but to pull down before the fire every way.

At last met my Lord Mayor in Canning Street, like a man spent, with a handkerchief about his neck. To the King's message he cried, like a fainting woman, "Lord! what can I do? I am spent: people will not obey me. I have been pulling down houses; but the fire overtakes us faster than we can do it." So he left me, and I him, and walked home, seeing people all almost distracted, and no manner of means used to quench the fire. The houses, too, so very thick thereabouts, and full of matter for burning, as pitch and tarr, in Thames Street; and warehouses of oil, and wines, and brandy, and other things.

Having seen as much as I could now, I away to Whitehall by appointment, and there walked to St. James' Park, and there met my wife and Creed and Wood and his wife, and walked to my boat; and there upon the water again, and to the fire up and down, it still increasing, and the wind great. So near the fire as we could for smoke; and all over the Thames, with one's face in the wind, you were almost burned with a shower of firedrops.

**Adapted from *The Diary of Samuel Pepys*
by Samuel Pepys**

6: *The Diary of Samuel Pepys*

Marks

These questions are all about *The Diary of Samuel Pepys* on pages 45 and 46.

Words in context

1. *I did see the houses at that end of the bridge all on fire, and an **infinite** great fire on this and the other side the end of the bridge*

   What does *infinite* mean in this sentence?

   _____

   1

2. *Everybody **endeavouring** to remove their goods*

   Circle **one** word that is closest in meaning to *endeavouring*.

   rushing   refusing   trying   wanting

   1

3. *The houses, too, so very **thick** thereabouts*

   Draw a line to join *thick* to its meaning in this sentence.

   thick

   fat
   wide
   strong
   dense

   1

6: *The Diary of Samuel Pepys*

Retrieval/identification

4. At what time did Pepys first hear of the fire?

_____

5. Which church was burned down?

_____

6. Where did Pepys meet his wife?

_____

Summarising main ideas

7. Number the events below to show the order in which they happen in the story. The first one has been done for you.

Jane wakes Pepys. [1]

Pepys meets the Lord Mayor. [ ]

Pepys visits the Lieutenant of the Tower. [ ]

Pepys is called to the King. [ ]

Pepys meets Creed and Wood. [ ]

6: *The Diary of Samuel Pepys*

Inference

8. From the first paragraph, **find** and **copy** the phrase that explains why Pepys thought the fire was far enough away for him to go to bed.

_____

Marks

1

9. Read the paragraph beginning *About seven rose again to dress myself*. Give **two** reasons why Pepys might have felt safer at this time.

1. _____

2. _____

2

10. Why might pulling down houses stop the fire?

_____

_____

1

11. Give **two** reasons why the Lord Mayor had failed to stop the fire.

1. _____

_____

2. _____

_____

2

6: *The Diary of Samuel Pepys*

Inference

12. How did the contents of the warehouses add to the fire?

_____

_____

1

13. In the last paragraph, Pepys returns to Whitehall *by appointment*. What is the likely reason for his visit?

_____

1

Prediction

14. With the wind *still increasing*, what is likely to happen to the fire?

_____

1

6: *The Diary of Samuel Pepys*

How information is related

15. Give **three** places that are mentioned twice in the extract.

1. _____

2. _____

3. _____

Marks

1

How meaning is enhanced

16. Read the final paragraph. **Find** and **copy one** phrase that shows how dangerous the fire was.

_____

_____

1

Making comparisons

17. How does Pepys' attitude towards the fire change during the extract?

_____

_____

_____

2

End of test

7: Hard Times

In this extract, the speaker is explaining to a teacher in a Victorian school what he thinks children's education should be like.

Chapter 1 – The one thing needful

"NOW, what I want is, Facts. Teach these boys and girls nothing but Facts. Facts alone are wanted in life. Plant nothing else, and root out everything else. You can only form the minds of reasoning animals upon Facts: nothing else will ever be of any service to them. This is the principle on which I bring up my own children, and this is the principle on which I bring up these children. Stick to Facts, sir!"

The scene was a plain, bare, monotonous vault of a school-room, and the speaker's square forefinger emphasized his observations by underscoring every sentence with a line on the schoolmaster's sleeve. The emphasis was helped by the speaker's square wall of a forehead, which had his eyebrows for its base, while his eyes found commodious cellarage in two dark caves, overshadowed by the wall. The emphasis was helped by the speaker's mouth, which was wide, thin, and hard set. The emphasis was helped by the speaker's voice, which was inflexible, dry, and dictatorial. The emphasis was helped by the speaker's hair, which bristled on the skirts of his bald head, a plantation of firs to keep the wind from its shining surface. The speaker's obstinate carriage, square coat, square legs, square shoulders all helped the emphasis.

"In this life, we want nothing but Facts, sir; nothing but Facts!"...

Chapter 2 – Murdering the innocents

THOMAS GRADGRIND, sir. A man of realities. A man of facts and calculations. A man who proceeds upon the principle that two and two are four, and nothing over, and who is not to be talked into allowing for anything over. Thomas Gradgrind, sir—peremptorily Thomas—Thomas Gradgrind. With a rule and a pair of scales, and the multiplication table always in his pocket, sir, ready to weigh and measure any parcel of human nature, and tell you exactly what it comes to. It is a mere question of figures, a case of simple arithmetic. You might hope to get some other nonsensical belief into the head of George Gradgrind, or Augustus Gradgrind, or John Gradgrind, or Joseph Gradgrind (all supposititious, non-existent persons), but into the head of Thomas Gradgrind—no, sir!

"Girl number twenty," said Mr. Gradgrind, squarely pointing with his square forefinger, "I don't know that girl. Who is that girl?"

"Sissy Jupe, sir," explained number twenty, blushing, standing up, and curtseying.

"Sissy is not a name," said Mr. Gradgrind. "Don't call yourself Sissy. Call yourself Cecilia."

7: Hard Times

"It's father as calls me Sissy, sir," returned the young girl in a trembling voice, and with another curtsey.

"Then he has no business to do it," said Mr. Gradgrind. "Tell him he mustn't. Cecilia Jupe. Let me see. What is your father?"

"He belongs to the horse-riding, if you please, sir."

Mr. Gradgrind frowned, and waved off the objectionable calling with his hand.

"We don't want to know anything about that, here. You mustn't tell us about that, here. Your father breaks horses, don't he?"

"If you please, sir, when they can get any to break, they do break horses in the ring, sir."

"You mustn't tell us about the ring, here. Very well, then. Describe your father as a horsebreaker. He doctors sick horses, I dare say?"

"Oh yes, sir."

"Very well, then. He is a veterinary surgeon, a farrier, and horsebreaker. Give me your definition of a horse."

(Sissy Jupe thrown into the greatest alarm by this demand.)

"Girl number twenty unable to define a horse!" said Mr. Gradgrind. "Girl number twenty possessed of no facts, in reference to one of the commonest of animals! Some boy's definition of a horse. Bitzer, yours."

The square finger, moving here and there, lighted suddenly on Bitzer. The boys and girls sat in two compact bodies, divided up the centre by a narrow interval; and Sissy, being at the corner of a row on the sunny side, came in for the beginning of a sunbeam, of which Bitzer, being at the corner of a row on the other side, a few rows in advance, caught the end. But, whereas the girl was so dark-eyed and dark-haired, that she seemed to receive a deeper and more lustrous colour from the sun, when it shone upon her, the boy was so light-eyed and light-haired that the self-same rays appeared to draw out of him what little colour he ever possessed. His cold eyes would hardly have been eyes, but for the short ends of lashes which, by bringing them into immediate contrast with something paler than themselves, expressed their form. His short-cropped hair might have been a mere continuation of the sandy freckles on his forehead and face. His skin was so unwholesomely deficient in the natural tinge, that he looked as though, if he were cut, he would bleed white.

"Bitzer," said Thomas Gradgrind. "Your definition of a horse."

"Quadruped. Graminivorous. Forty teeth, namely twenty-four grinders, four eye-teeth, and twelve incisive. Sheds coat in the spring; in marshy countries, sheds hoofs, too. Hoofs hard, but requiring to be shod with iron. Age known by marks in mouth." Thus (and much more) Bitzer.

"Now girl number twenty," said Mr. Gradgrind. "You know what a horse is."

She curtseyed again, and would have blushed deeper, if she could have blushed deeper than she had blushed all this time.

**Extract from *Hard Times*
by Charles Dickens**

7: Hard Times

These questions are all about *Hard Times* on pages 52 and 53.

Words in context

1. *The scene was a plain, bare, monotonous vault of a school-room.*

    Circle the word that tells us that the school-room was very large.

    | plain | bare | monotonous | vault |

    Marks: 1

2. *Thomas Gradgrind. With a **rule** and a pair of scales, and the multiplication table always in his pocket*

    Draw a link to join *rule* to its meaning in this extract.

    rule — law / regulation / ruler / direction

    Marks: 1

3. How many legs does a *quadruped* have?

    Tick **one**.

    one ☐   three ☐
    two ☐   four ☐

    Marks: 1

7: Hard Times

Retrieval/identification

4. What, according to Thomas Gradgrind, are the only things wanted in life?

_____

Marks: 1

5. Put a tick in the correct box to show whether each of the following statements about Thomas Gradgrind is **true** or **false**.

	True	False
He had a large forehead.		
His eyes were in bright sockets.		
His mouth was narrow.		
His shoulders were square.		

Marks: 1

6. From the paragraph beginning THOMAS GRADGRIND, sir, **find** and **copy** the names of **four** non-existent persons.

_____   _____

_____   _____

Marks: 1

7. What does Gradgrind say Sissy should call herself?

_____

Marks: 1

7: Hard Times

Retrieval/identification

8. Give **one** of the occupations that Gradgrind says Sissy's father has.

_____

9. According to Bitzer, how many incisive teeth does a horse have?

_____

10. According to Bitzer, what tells us the age of a horse?

_____

Summarising main ideas

11. Number the events below to show the order in which they happen in the story. The first one has been done for you.

Gradgrind tells the teacher that children only need facts. `1`

Sissy curtseys for the third time. ☐

Bitzer gives a definition of a horse. ☐

Gradgrind tells Sissy to call herself Cecilia. ☐

Gradgrind asks Sissy to give a definition of a horse. ☐

7: *Hard Times*

Inference

12. *The emphasis was helped by the speaker's voice, which was inflexible, dry, and dictatorial.*

Give **three** things that this tells us about Gradgrind's character.

1. _____
2. _____
3. _____

13. Gradgrind calls Sissy, *Girl number twenty.* Give **three** things this might tell us about Victorian education.

1. _____
2. _____
3. _____

14. In the paragraph beginning *The square finger*, Bitzer's skin is *unwholesomely deficient in the natural tinge.* Explain why this might have made him look *as though, if he were cut, he would bleed white.*

_____
_____
_____

Marks

3

3

2

7: Hard Times

Inference

15. Read the final sentence. Give **one** reason why the girl could not *have blushed deeper than she had blushed all this time.*

_____

_____

_____

1

Prediction

16. What is likely to happen if Sissy is asked again by Gradgrind to give a definition of a horse? Give a reason for your answer.

_____

_____

_____

2

How information is related

17. (Sissy Jupe thrown into the greatest alarm by this demand.)

How does this sentence link to the end of the extract?

_____

_____

1

7: Hard Times

Marks

How meaning is enhanced

18. *the speaker's square forefinger emphasized his observations*

> This sentence appears in the second paragraph. The author then uses the phrase *The emphasis was helped by* in the same paragraph. Explain how he uses the phrase and why.

_____

_____

2

Making comparisons

19. In the paragraph beginning, *The square finger*, how does the light affect the appearance of Sissy and Bitzer?

_____

_____

_____

2

End of test

8: Brazil

History

Time has not always been kind to Brazil. As far as Europe was concerned, it did not exist before 1500, yet it had a population of about seven million people. All of that changed with the arrival of the Portuguese, who conquered the country, took control of it and started to strip it of its treasures and other assets. Nowadays, Brazil is the fifth-largest country in the world by area and has Portuguese as one of its official languages. The name 'Brazil' seems to come from the brazilwood, a tree that once grew plentifully along the Brazilian coast.

Brazil declared itself independent of Portugal in 1822. This led to the Brazilian War of Independence which continued until 1824, with Portugal officially recognising Brazil as a separate country in 1825.

There was a government but for more than 50 of the first 100 years of republic in Brazil, the army was in control. It has regularly taken power and then released it back to the people. The latest intervention was as recently as the 1960s. The army maintained control until the 1980s when democratic elections were held once more.

Law and order

In relation to the rest of the world, Brazil still has above-average levels of crime, particularly gun crime. In 2012, the World Health Organization said that Brazil had one of the highest murder rates in the world. Large amounts of money have been invested in recruiting additional police officers. Perhaps strangely, the crime rate is not the same in all areas of the country. For example, it is four times higher in Alagoas than it is in São Paulo. To go with this, Brazil has one of the highest levels of prison populations in the world.

It is not surprising that some people questioned the wisdom of taking the Olympics there in 2016. Fortunately, nothing serious happened and the Olympics were a great success.

8: Brazil

Economy
Brazil has the largest economy in South America but it has changed considerably from its early days. Originally its main export was sugar cane but it has been the world's largest coffee producer for over 150 years. It now has a mixed economy using its natural resources in agriculture, mining and manufacturing as well as its service industries like tourism.

Tourism
With the advent of cheap flights, tourism is growing rapidly in Brazil and is a major part of the economy. Only Mexico and Argentina have more visitors per year in Central and South America.

People come for the natural areas like the River Amazon and the equatorial rain forests. They are also drawn by the beaches and nightlife of places like Copacabana in Rio.

Sport
It is impossible to think of Brazil without thinking of football. The Brazilian national team is always a major contender in international competitions like the World Cup. People are drawn to the 'samba style' and entertainment of the team. Combining high skill levels and a philosophy of attacking play, it is little wonder that Brazil has won the World Cup five times.

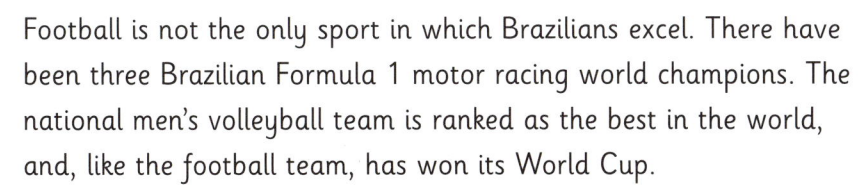

Football is not the only sport in which Brazilians excel. There have been three Brazilian Formula 1 motor racing world champions. The national men's volleyball team is ranked as the best in the world, and, like the football team, has won its World Cup.

The future
What does the future hold for Brazil? It is hard to say. Its economy has great strengths but it has also gone through several recessions so there is no guarantee that it will thrive. Balanced against this are large areas of deep poverty, contrasting with areas of opulent, excessive wealth. In sport, can Brazil maintain its position as a world leader when it has so many social problems at home? It is a problem that the government will have to balance. For the rest of the world, Brazil is a beautiful, exciting country. As South America opens up to a second European invasion, will it be able to cope or will the levels of crime mean that the visitors go elsewhere? Only time will tell.

8: *Brazil*

These questions are all about *Brazil* on pages 60 and 61.

Words in context

1. The first paragraph talks about Brazil's *treasures and other* **assets**.

   What does *assets* mean in this phrase?

   _____

   Marks: 1

2. *Combining high skill levels and a* **philosophy** *of attacking play*

   Circle **one** word that is closest in meaning to *philosophy*.

   | opposition | resistance | policy | commitment |

   Marks: 1

3. *large areas of deep poverty, contrasting with areas of* **opulent**, *excessive wealth*

   Draw a line to join *opulent* to its meaning in this sentence.

   opulent

   impoverished

   lavish

   poor

   obvious

   Marks: 1

8: Brazil

Retrieval/identification

Marks

4. How is it likely that Brazil got its name?

_____

1

5. Where is the crime rate four times higher than São Paulo?

_____

1

6. Give **two** countries in Central and South America that have more visitors than Brazil.

1. _____

2. _____

1

Summarising main ideas

7. Number the events below to show the order in which they happened. The first one has been done for you.

The Portuguese discover Brazil.	1
The army takes control for the final time.	☐
The Brazilian War of Independence takes place.	☐
The Olympics are held in Brazil.	☐
The World Health Organization says Brazil has one of the highest murder rates in the world.	☐

1

8: *Brazil*

Inference

8. Give **one** reason why Brazil did not exist for Europeans before 1500.

_____

Marks

1

9. Read the section headed 'Law and order'. Give **three** reasons why Brazil might have a large prison population.

1. _____

_____

2. _____

_____

3. _____

_____

3

10. Give **one** reason why some people might have questioned the wisdom of holding the Olympics in Brazil.

_____

_____

1

11. Give **one** reason why tourism is increasing rapidly in Brazil.

_____

_____

1

Inference

12. Give **three** reasons why it is hard to say what the future will hold for Brazil.

1. _____

2. _____

3. _____

Marks: 3

13. *As South America opens up to a second European invasion*

What are the two 'invasions' that the author is referring to in the final paragraph?

1. _____

2. _____

Marks: 2

Prediction

14. Read the final paragraph. What is likely to happen to Brazil's tourist industry in the future? Give a reason for your answer.

_____

_____

_____

Marks: 2

8: *Brazil*

How information is related

15. Give **one** way that the final sentence links to the first one.

_____

_____

Marks

1

How meaning is enhanced

16. Read the final section. **Find** and **copy one** statement that shows how difficult it will be for the government to make decisions about how to develop Brazil.

_____

_____

1

Making comparisons

17. How has Brazil's economy changed over the years?

1. _____

2. _____

3. _____

3

End of test

9: Robinson Crusoe

CHAPTER I

—

START IN LIFE

I was born in the year 1632, in the city of York, of a good family, though not of that country, my father being a foreigner of Bremen, who settled first at Hull. He got a good estate by merchandise, and leaving off his trade, lived afterwards at York, from whence he had married my mother, whose relations were named Robinson, a very good family in that country, and from whom I was called Robinson Kreutznaer; but, by the usual corruption of words in England, we are now called—nay we call ourselves and write our name—Crusoe; and so my companions always called me.

I had two elder brothers, one of whom was lieutenant-colonel to an English regiment of foot in Flanders, formerly commanded by the famous Colonel Lockhart, and was killed at the battle near Dunkirk against the Spaniards. What became of my second brother I never knew, any more than my father or mother knew what became of me.

Being the third son of the family and not bred to any trade, my head began to be filled very early with rambling thoughts. My father, who was very ancient, had given me a competent share of learning, as far as house-education and a country free school generally go, and designed me for the law; but I would be satisfied with nothing but going to sea; and my inclination to this led me so strongly against the will, nay, the commands of my father, and against all the entreaties and persuasions of my mother and other friends, that there seemed to be something fatal in that propensity of nature, tending directly to the life of misery which was to befall me.

My father, a wise and grave man, gave me serious and excellent counsel against what he foresaw was my design.

I took my mother at a time when I thought her a little more pleasant than ordinary, and told her that my thoughts were so entirely bent upon seeing the world that I should never settle to anything with resolution enough to go through with it, and my father had better give me his consent than force me to go without it; that I was now eighteen years old, which was too late to go apprentice to a trade or clerk to an attorney; that I was sure if I did I should never serve out my time, but I should certainly run away from my master before my time was

9: Robinson Crusoe

out, and go to sea; and if she would speak to my father to let me go one voyage abroad, if I came home again, and did not like it, I would go no more; and I would promise, by a double diligence, to recover the time that I had lost.

Though my mother refused to move it to my father, yet I heard afterwards that she reported all the discourse to him, and that my father, after showing a great concern at it, said to her, with a sigh, "That boy might be happy if he would stay at home; but if he goes abroad, he will be the most miserable wretch that ever was born: I can give no consent to it."

On the 1st of September 1651, I went on board a ship bound for London. Never any young adventurer's misfortunes, I believe, began sooner, or continued longer than mine. The ship was no sooner out of the Humber than the wind began to blow and the sea to rise in a most frightful manner; and, as I had never been at sea before, I was most inexpressibly sick in body and terrified in mind. I began now seriously to reflect upon what I had done, and how justly I was overtaken by the judgment of Heaven for my wicked leaving my father's house, and abandoning my duty. All the good counsels of my parents, my father's tears and my mother's entreaties, came now fresh into my mind; and my conscience, which was not yet come to the pitch of hardness to which it has since, reproached me with the contempt of advice, and the breach of my duty to God and my father.

All this while the storm increased, and the sea went very high, though nothing like what I have seen many times since; no, nor what I saw a few days after; but it was enough to affect me then, who was but a young sailor, and had never known anything of the matter. I expected every wave would have swallowed us up, and that every time the ship fell down, as I thought it did, in the trough or hollow of the sea, we should never rise more; in this agony of mind, I made many vows and resolutions that if it would please God to spare my life in this one voyage, if ever I got once my foot upon dry land again, I would go directly home to my father, and never set it into a ship again while I lived; that I would take his advice, and never run myself into such miseries as these any more.

Adapted from *The Life and Adventures of Robinson Crusoe* by Daniel Defoe

9: *Robinson Crusoe*

These questions are all about *Robinson Crusoe* on pages 67 and 68.

Words in context

1. *I would be satisfied with nothing but going to sea; and my* **inclination** *to this led me so strongly against the will, nay, the commands of my father*

   Draw a line to join *inclination* to its meaning in this sentence.

   inclination

   steepness

   leaning

   hatred

   opposition

   1

2. *Never any young adventurer's* **misfortunes**, *I believe, began sooner, or continued longer than mine.*

   What does *misfortunes* mean in this sentence?

   _____

   1

9: Robinson Crusoe

Words in context

3. *I was most **inexpressibly** sick in body*

   Circle **one** word that is closest in meaning to *inexpressibly*.

   remarkably | indescribably | terribly | alarmingly

   Marks: 1

Retrieval/identification

4. Where did Robinson's father first settle?

   _____

   1

5. Who was Robinson's brother fighting against when he was killed?

   _____

   1

6. How old was Robinson when he went to sea?

   _____

   1

7. On what date did Robinson set sail for London?

   _____

   1

9: Robinson Crusoe

Summarising main ideas

Marks

8. Number the events below to show the order in which they happen in the story. The first one has been done for you.

Robinson's family move to York. `1`

Robinson tries to persuade his mother to talk to his father. ☐

The storm takes place. ☐

The ship leaves the River Humber. ☐

Robinson's father advises him not to go to sea. ☐

1

Inference

9. Give **two** reasons why Robinson's family might have called themselves 'Crusoe'.

1. _____

2. _____

2

10. From the paragraph 2 beginning *I had two elder brothers*, **find** and **copy** the sentence that tells us Robinson never returned home.

_____

_____

_____

1

9: Robinson Crusoe

Inference

11. From the paragraph beginning *Being the third son of the family*, how does the writer show that the father was more against the boy going to sea than his mother was?

   _____

   _____

   _____

   2

12. Give **two** reasons why Robinson might have asked his mother to talk to his father rather than do it himself.

   1. _____

   2. _____

   2

Prediction

13. What is likely to happen to Robinson's ship at the end of the extract? Give a reason for your answer.

   _____

   _____

   _____

   2

9: *Robinson Crusoe*

Marks

How information is related

14. *"That boy might be happy if he would stay at home; but if he goes abroad, he will be the most miserable wretch that ever was born"*

Give **three** ways that the father's prediction of misery links to the rest of the extract.

1. _____
2. _____
3. _____

3

How meaning is enhanced

15. Read the final paragraph. **Find** and **copy two** phrases that increase the tension in the story.

1. _____
2. _____

2

Making comparisons

16. How does Robinson's attitude towards his father change during the extract?

_____
_____
_____

2

End of test

Answers

The answers are given below. The answers usually only include the information the children are expected to give. There may be some places where the answers vary or multiple answers are acceptable, these are marked as such. Note that in some places, answers will be varied and subjective from child to child, and a fair degree of marker discretion and interpretation is needed, particularly if children's understanding and skills have to be deduced from their answers.

Q	Answers	Marks
1: *Oscar to the Rescue* (pages 8–15)		
1	**Award 1 mark** for: any answers that make reference to covering the footprints up or destroying the footprints, or similar.	1
2	**Award 1 mark** for: fated	1
3	**Award 1 mark** for: unnoticeably	1
4	**Award 1 mark** for both: • The weather changed. • The was someone waiting for Oscar.	1
5	**Award 1 mark** for: answers that refer to the landslide. Possible alternatives include: • A terrible landslide. • They were swept away in a terrible landslide.	1
6	**Award 1 mark** for both: • a torch • a dog whistle **Do not award** any marks for *a long silver tube* or just *a whistle* as neither of these is precise enough.	1
7	**Award 3 marks** for any three of: • He is the only one who can save the children. • He climbs the mountain to find the children. • He carries on, even though he does not know where he is going. • He is not worried about his own safety. **Award 2 marks** for any two of the above. **Award 1 mark** for any of the above. Accept also any other reasonable suggestions.	3
8	**Award 1 mark** for: loomed, forebodingly, ominously	1
9	**Award 1 mark** for either of: • This was the way it always happened. • It had happened before so he knew what to expect.	1
10	**Award 2 marks** for any two of: • The snow was up to Oscar's waist. • It would have been very deep for the dog to go through. • The slope was very steep. • The snow might have been slippery. **Award 1 mark** for one of the above.	2
11	**Award 2 marks** for: • The snow had covered all of the tracks. • It was too dark to see much. **Award 1 mark** for one of the above.	2

Answers

Q	Answers	Marks
1: *Oscar to the Rescue* (pages 8–15) continued		
12	**Award 2 marks** for: • The man in black had not come with him. • He had lost Kaiser. **Award 1 mark** for one of the above.	2
13	**Award 2 marks** for reasonable answers that include an explanation. For example: • Oscar is likely to find the children because he seems to have done this kind of thing before. • Oscar and Kaiser will find other things to help them find the children, or similar. **Award 1 mark** for answers that give a reasonable prediction but do not include an explanation. **Do not award** any marks for answers that suggest that Oscar will fail. That would be against the nature of this genre.	2
14	**Award 1 mark** for answers that show understanding of the ending of each chapter being a cliffhanger.	1
15	**Award 2 marks** for answers that explain: • calling the event *it* makes the reader think that whatever will happen will be very strange • emphasising *would* gives it more strength and makes the reader know that it will certainly happen. **Award 1 mark** for either of the above.	2
16	**Award 2 marks** for any two of: • At first he is an ordinary little boy, taking his dog for a walk • At the end he is a brave hero trying to save the children • At the start he is not in control • At the end he has taken control **Award 1 mark** for any of the above.	2
2: *Icarus and Daedalus* (pages 16–23)		
1	**Award 1 mark** for: wicked	1
2	**Award 1 mark** for: any answers that show understanding that 'surreptitiously' means secretly, or words with similar meanings.	1
3	**Award 1 mark** for: fragile	1
4	**Award 1 mark** for both of: buildings and temples	1
5	**Award 1 mark** for: Icarus was out of earshot or Icarus was too far away to hear.	1
6	**Award 1 mark** for all correct: 		True	False
Daedalus was definitely the finest architect of his time.		✓
You will certainly have heard of Minos.		✓
Daedalus' wings were made from feathers and wax.	✓	
Daedalus tried to warn Icarus about the sun.	✓			1
7	**Award 3 marks** for: • When he did not dare tell Minos what he thought about the Minotaur. • When he feared torture. • When he was too scared to look back at the end. **Award 2 marks** for any two of the above. **Award 1 mark** for any of the above.	3
8	**Award 1 mark** for: he didn't think that it was right to have a monster that ate people.	1

Answers

Q	Answers	Marks
2: *Icarus and Daedalus* (pages 16–23) continued		
9	**Award 2 marks** for: • Daedalus had designed the Labyrinth so he knew the way in and out. • No one else knew the way in or out. **Award 1 mark** for either of the above.	2
10	**Award 1 mark** for: to reward Daedalus for his work on the Labyrinth.	1
11	**Award 2 marks** for any two of: • It seemed obvious that Daedalus was guilty as no one else knew their way through the intricate tunnel system. • Minos could not believe that Theseus could have found his way in and out without help. • Minos could not see another answer. • Theseus had left the island so he could not tell Minos what had happened. • It was too dangerous for Theseus to return to clear Daedalus' name. • There was no one who could support Daedalus' side of the story. **Award 1 mark** for any of the above.	2
12	**Award 3 marks** for: • He felt responsible for Icarus' death. • He had taken Icarus to Crete. • He had designed/made the wings. **Award 2 marks** for any two of the above. **Award 1 mark** for any of the above.	3
13	**Award 2 marks** for: • Icarus was dead. • He could not go back to Crete. **Award 1 mark** for either of the above.	2
14	**Award 1 mark** for any reasonable answers that fit what we know about Minos' character from the text. Possible acceptable suggestions include: • He might punish the guards for letting them escape. • He might send soldiers after them to bring them back.	1
15	**Award 2 marks** for answers that relate *designed* back to the story in two ways: • If he hadn't been a good designer, he would never have been to Crete. • If he hadn't designed the Labyrinth, Icarus would still be alive. **Award 1 mark** for any one of the above.	2
16	**Award 1 mark** for: He expected to be tortured mercilessly	1
17	**Award 2 marks** for: • At first Minos thought Daedalus was wonderful because he designed the Labyrinth. • Later he thought that Daedalus was a traitor. **Award 1 mark** for either of the above.	2
3: *The Charge of the Light Brigade* (pages 24–29)		
1	**Award 1 mark** for: any answers that make reference to making a mistake or similar.	1
2	**Award 1 mark** for: respect	1
3	**Award 1 mark** for: splendid	1
4	**Award 1 mark** for: the guns	1
5	**Award 1 mark** for all three: • to the right of them • to the left of them • in front of them.	1

Answers

Q	Answers	Marks
3: *The Charge of the Light Brigade* (pages 24–29) continued		
6	**Award 1 mark** for both: Cossack and Russian	1
7	**Award 1 mark** for all numbered correctly: The light Brigade is ordered to attack. 1 The soldiers used their sabres. 4 The Light Brigade rode back from the mouth of Hell. 5 The soldiers do not question their order. 2 The Light Brigade rode into the jaws of Death. 3	1
8	**Award 1 mark** for any three of: • Not though the soldier knew • Someone had blundered • Theirs not to make reply • Theirs not to reason why • Theirs but to do and die	1
9	**Award 3 marks** for any three of: • It was shaped like a mouth • Once the soldiers were in, the jaws could close behind them • It could swallow the soldiers • Lots of people would die there **Award 2 marks** for any two of the above. **Award 1 mark** for any one of the above.	3
10	**Award 1 mark** for either of: • Everyone wondered why they were attacking cannons with horses and swords. • Everyone wondered what would happen to them.	1
11	**Award 1 mark**s for: hero	1
12	**Award 1 mark** for: all that was left of them	1
13	**Award 1 mark** for: answers that show understanding of the poet's intention to glorify the soldiers.	1
14	**Award 1 mark** for any reasonable response such as: • It was heroic because they rode against cannons with only swords as their weapons. • It was stupid to ride against cannons with only swords as weapons. • The soldiers' lives were wasted.	1
15	**Award 1 mark** for: by repeating 600 at the end of each verse.	1
16	**Award 2 marks** for any two of: • It was a mixture of shells and bullets. • There was a large amount of it. • It was as thick as a heavy rainstorm. **Award 1 mark** for any of the above.	2
17	**Award 2 marks** for: • At first the cannons were to the left, right and in front of them. • At the end the cannons were to the left, right and behind them. **Award 1 mark** for either of the above.	2
4: *Wheelchair Warrior* (pages 30–37)		
1	**Award 1 mark** for: any answers that make reference to confusion or similar.	1
2	**Award 1 mark** for: eyeshade	1
3	**Award 1 mark** for: stop	1

Answers

Q	Answers	Marks
4: *Wheelchair Warrior* (pages 30–37) continued		
4	**Award 1 mark** for: as carefully as a bomb disposal expert would a lethal minefield	1
5	**Award 2 marks** for: • coming up the last slope and reaching the top of the hill • the bike taking off as he rode the jump • the sunlight glaring across his visor. **Award 1 mark** for any two of the above. **Do not award** any marks for *The last thing he could remember was the race, the final one of the season*, as this was not immediately before the crash.	2
6	**Award 1 mark** for any three of: • The swish of the door • The click of his mother's heels • His mother's heels slowing down • His mother sobbing quietly.	1
7	**Award 2 marks** for any three of: • It's too early to say how well he is doing • He might never walk again • It's really a case now of wait and see • He will be able to hear her speak • He will be aware that she is there. **Award 1 mark** for any two of the above.	2
8	**Award 1 mark** for any of: • They did not want Elliott to hear them. • They did not want other patients to hear them. • It was a difficult conversation.	1
9	**Award 2 marks** for any two of: • He blacked out before the crash. • He has lost his memory. • He doesn't want to remember. **Award 1 mark** for any of the above.	2
10	**Award 2 marks** for any two of: • It was hard to give her bad news. • He did not want to upset her. • It was a complex injury. • Elliott's injuries were difficult to understand. • He did not know how bad Elliott's injuries were. • He did not want to give her false hope. **Award 1 mark** for any of the above.	2
11	**Award 3 marks** for any three appropriate reasons such as: • He thought it would be worse to delay the news. • It was bad news. • He wanted to get it over with quickly. • He was too busy to spend a long time explaining. • He wanted Elliott's mother to understand easily. **Award 2 marks** for any two of the above. **Award 1 mark** for any one of the above.	3
12	**Award 1 mark** for: answers that show understanding that the monitors will tell them.	1
13	**Award 1 mark** for any of: • Elliott does not know where he is. • Elliott does not remember the crash. • Elliott does not know why his mother is leaving him. • Elliott does not know what 'this' is.	1

Answers

Q	Answers	Marks
4: *Wheelchair Warrior* (pages 30–37) continued		
14	**Award 1 mark** for any of: • The doctors will run further tests/give further treatment. • The monitors will tell the doctors something is happening. • Elliott will recover. • Elliott will never be able to walk again. • Elliott will be in a wheelchair.	1
15	**Award 3 marks** for any three of: • When he doesn't know where he is. • When he doesn't know why his mother is talking to a doctor. • When the doctor talks about 'he'. • When his mother leaves. **Award 2 marks** for any two of the above. **Award 1 mark** for any of the above.	3
16	**Award 2 marks** for any two of: • He can think but he can't move. • He feels trapped inside it. • His brain is unable to get messages to the rest of his body. **Award 1 mark** for any of the above.	2
17	**Award 2 marks** for any of the following: • It was difficult because the memory was hiding. • It was hard to get to the memory because he had to prise it out. • He could only get the memory out gradually or he could not get the memory out in one go.	2
18	**Award 2 marks** for accurate descriptions such as: • At first he did not understand where he was or why he was there. At the end he knew what was happening. • At first he lay in his bed, doing nothing. At the end he was trying to communicate.	2
5: *Skiathos* (pages 38–44)		
1	**Award 1 mark** for: any answers that make reference to *genuine*, *real* or similar.	1
2	**Award 1 mark** for: customers **Do not award** any marks for *tourists*. It does fit the meaning of the sentence but it does not have the sense of clients that *customers* does.	1
3	**Award 1 mark** for: original	1
4	**Award 1 mark** for both of: Ferries and fast catamarans **Do not award** any marks for *water taxi*. In the extract it only sails to Skiathos town and back, not to other islands.	1
5	**Award 1 mark** for: • The island is so small that it's not worth it • the bus service is so good that you'll find you don't need your own transport.	1
6	**Award 2 marks** for: • to leave the airport • to go to the taverna across the road. **Award 1 mark** for any of the above.	2

Answers

Q	Answers			Marks
\multicolumn{4}{l	}{**5: *Skiathos* (pages 38–44) continued**}	

Q	Answers	True	False	Marks
7	**Award 1 mark** for all correct:			1
	Skiathos is an island in the Sporades.	✓		
	The beaches of Troulos and Agia Paraskevi are aimed at young people.		✓	
	The bus will take you from Koukounaries to Skiathos town for about two euros.	✓		
	Planes fly low over the town to land at the airport.	✓		
8	**Award 1 mark** for any answer that suggests you might be too interested or enjoying yourself too much to leave. Acceptable alternatives include: • You might want to carry on shopping. • You might want to continue exploring the cobbled streets.			1
9	**Award 2 marks** for any two of: • They are hard to get to. • You need to hire transport. • Most people think it is too difficult to walk to them. **Award 1 mark** for any of the above.			2
10	**Award 1 mark** for any of: • There will be few tourists so it is not needed as much. • There will only be locals on the island so it will not be needed as much.			1
11	**Award 2 marks** for any two of: • It would frighten passengers. • It would put passengers off flying from there. • No one took any pictures of crashes. • There haven't been any crashes. **Award 1 mark** for any of the above.			2
12	**Award 1 mark** for any reasonable answer. For example: • There will be nothing for you to find out. • You might not want to go.			1
13	**Award 1 mark** for: You will fall in love with the island, or similar.			1
14	**Award 2 marks** for: • They will return to Skiathos. • They will visit the other islands. **Award 1 mark** for either of the above.			2
15	**Award 3 marks** for: • The first section says most people don't go past Skiathos. The final one encourages people to go to the other islands. • The first section talks about the charm of the other islands. The final one says to tell you more would spoil it for you. • They both mention the boomerang. **Award 2 marks** for any two of the above. **Award 1 mark** for any of the above or answers that show a link but do not give any evidence.			3
16	**Award 2 marks** for any two of: • Most people go to sunbathe. • The sun-burned tourists are red like lobsters. • Lobsters are crammed together in pots when caught. **Award 1 mark** for any of the above.			2
17	**Award 3 marks** for any three of: • They do not have airports. • They have fewer tourists. • They are quieter. • They are more relaxed. • They are not usually visited by tourists on their first trip. **Award 2 marks** for any two of the above. **Award 1 mark** for any of the above.			3

Answers

Q	Answers	Marks
6: *The Diary of Samuel Pepys* (pages 45–51)		
1	**Award 1 mark** for: any answers that make reference to *endless* or similar.	1
2	**Award 1 mark** for: trying	1
3	**Award 1 mark** for: dense	1
4	**Award 1 mark** for: about three in the morning	1
5	**Award 1 mark** for: St Magnus'	1
6	**Award 1 mark** for: St. James' Park	1
7	**Award 1 mark** for: Jane wakes Pepys. 1 Pepys meets the Lord Mayor. 4 Pepys visits the Lieutenant of the Tower. 2 Pepys is called to the King. 3 Pepys meets Creed and Wood. 5	1
8	**Award 1 mark** for: being unused to such fires as followed	1
9	**Award 2 marks** for: • He thought the fire was not as bad as before. • He thought the fire had moved further away. **Award 1 mark** for either of the above.	2
10	**Award 1 mark** for answers that show understanding that it would make gaps that the fire couldn't jump or similar.	1
11	**Award 2 marks** for any two of: • He was exhausted – *spent*. • People were refusing to obey him. • The fire was overtaking them faster than they could put it out. **Award 1 mark** for any of the above.	2
12	**Award 1 mark** for: answers that show understanding that all of the contents burned easily.	1
13	**Award 1 mark** for: to report back to the King.	1
14	**Award 1 mark** for: it will get stronger, or similar.	1
15	**Award 1 mark** for any three of: • The City • Fish Street • Whitehall • The Steelyard. **Do not award** any marks for *Tower* – the second reference is to the Lieutenant of the Tower, not the place. **Do not award** any marks for *Thames* – the first reference is *Thames Street*. The second reference is to the river.	1
16	**Award 1 mark** for: you were almost burned with a shower of firedrops	1
17	**Award 2 marks** for: • At first he was not worried by it. • At the end he realised how dangerous it was. **Award 1 mark** for either of the above.	2

Answers

Q	Answers	Marks
7: *Hard Times* (pages 52–59)		
1	**Award 1 mark** for: vault	1
2	**Award 1 mark** for: ruler	1
3	**Award 1 mark** for: four	1
4	**Award 1 mark** for: Facts	1
5	**Award 1 mark** for: <table><tr><th></th><th>True</th><th>False</th></tr><tr><td>He had a large forehead.</td><td>✓</td><td></td></tr><tr><td>His eyes were in bright sockets.</td><td></td><td>✓</td></tr><tr><td>His mouth was narrow.</td><td></td><td>✓</td></tr><tr><td>His shoulders were square.</td><td>✓</td><td></td></tr></table>	1
6	**Award 1 mark** for all four of: • George Gradgrind • Augustus Gradgrind • John Gradgrind • Joseph Gradgrind.	1
7	**Award 1 mark** for: Cecilia	1
8	**Award 1 mark** for any of: veterinary surgeon, a farrier or a horsebreaker.	1
9	**Award 1 mark** for: twelve	1
10	**Award 1 mark** for: marks in its mouth	1
11	**Award 1 mark** for: Gradgrind tells the teacher that children only need facts. 1 Sissy curtseys for the third time. 5 Bitzer gives a definition of a horse. 4 Gradgrind tells Sissy to call herself Cecilia. 2 Gradgrind asks Sissy to give a definition of a horse. 3	1
12	**Award 3 marks** for answers that correctly infer the implications of *inflexible, dry and dictatorial*, such as: • He did not change his mind a lot. • He was not interesting to listen to. • He liked telling people what to do. **Award 2 marks** for any two of the above. **Award 1 mark** for any of the above.	3
13	**Award 3 marks** for: • There were a lot of children in the class. • The children are not seen as individuals. • The teachers did not know all of the pupils' names. **Award 2 marks** for any two of the above. **Award 1 mark** for any of the above.	3
14	**Award 2 marks** for an explanation that includes: • His skin was very pale. • The colour of his skin made it seem like his blood would be the same. **Award 1 mark** for either of the above.	2

Answers

Q	Answers	Marks
7: *Hard Times* (pages 52–59) continued		
15	**Award 1 mark** for: answers that explain that the girl had already been completely embarrassed.	1
16	**Award 2 marks** for answers that include a reasonable prediction and an explanation. Possible acceptable answers include: • She will repeat Bitzer's definition because she thinks it is correct. • She will not give a definition because she cannot remember Bitzer's. • She will not give a definition because she will still be embarrassed. **Award 1 mark** for answers that include a reasonable prediction but do not give a reason.	2
17	**Award 1 mark** for answers that explain that Sissy's alarm is shown in her embarrassment and/or blushing.	1
18	**Award 2 marks** for: • The phrase is repeated a number of times. • To add an extra part of his features to build up a full picture. **Award 1 mark** for either of the above.	2
19	**Award 2 marks** for: • Sissy seemed to go darker and • Bitzer seemed to go lighter. Accept also the quotations: • she seemed to receive a deeper and more lustrous colour from the sun, when it shone upon her • the boy was so light-eyed and light-haired that the self-same rays appeared to draw out of him what little colour he ever possessed. **Award 1 mark** for any one of the above.	2
8: *Brazil* (pages 60–66)		
1	**Award 1 mark** for: any answers that make reference to valuable possessions, resources, belongings, goods or similar.	1
2	**Award 1 mark** for: policy	1
3	**Award 1 mark** for: lavish	1
4	**Award 1 mark** for: from the Brazilwood tree	1
5	**Award 1 mark** for: Alagoas	1
6	**Award 1 mark** for both of: Mexico and Argentina	1
7	**Award 1 mark** for: The Portuguese discover Brazil. 1 The army takes control for the final time. 3 The Brazilian War of Independence takes place. 2 The Olympics are held in Brazil. 5 The World Health Organisation says Brazil has one of the highest murder rates in the world. 4	1
8	**Award 1 mark** for: It had not been discovered by Europeans.	1

Answers

Q	Answers	Marks
8: *Brazil* (pages 60–66) continued		
9	**Award 3 marks** for any three of: • There is a high crime rate. • It has one of the highest murder rates in the world. • There has been a large investment to increase the number of police officers. • The increased numbers of police means that more criminals are being caught. **Award 2 marks** for any two of the above. **Award 1 mark** for any one of the above.	3
10	**Award 1 mark** for answers that show understanding that the crime rate made it dangerous for the athletes and the visitors, or similar.	1
11	**Award 1 mark** for: cheap flights	1
12	**Award 3 marks** for any three of: • Its economy has great strengths but there is no guarantee that it will thrive. • There are large areas of deep poverty contrasting with areas of opulent, excessive wealth. • It has so many social problems at home. • Crime levels might mean tourists will go elsewhere. **Award 2 marks** for any two of the above. **Award 1 mark** for any one of the above.	3
13	**Award 2 marks** for: • The first was the Portuguese conquering the country. • The second is European tourists coming to visit. **Award 1 mark** for either of the above.	2
14	**Award 2 marks** for answers that make a realistic prediction and support it with a reason. For example: • It will decline because the levels of crime will make people want to go somewhere safer. • It will increase because it is a beautiful, exciting country. **Award 1 mark** for answers that make a realistic prediction but do not support it with a reason.	2
15	**Award 1 mark** for answers such as: • They both refer to time. • They both suggest uncertainty about the future.	1
16	**Award 1 mark** for: It is a problem that the government will have to balance.	1
17	**Award 3 marks** for answers that include the following points: • At first sugar cane was the main export. • Brazil has been the world's largest producer of coffee for over 150 years. • Brazil now has a mixed economy. **Award 2 marks** for any two of the above. **Award 1 mark** for any one of the above.	3
9: *Robinson Crusoe* (pages 67–73)		
1	**Award 1 mark** for: leaning	1
2	**Award 1 mark** for: any answers that refer to bad luck or unfortunate events.	1
3	**Award 1 mark** for: indescribably	1
4	**Award 1 mark** for: Hull	1
5	**Award 1 mark** for: the Spaniards, the Spanish or Spain	1
6	**Award 1 mark** for: Eighteen	1

Answers

Q	Answers	Marks
9: *Robinson Crusoe* (pages 67–73) continued		
7	**Award 1 mark** for: 1st of September 1651	1
8	**Award 1 mark** for: Robinson's family move to York. 1 Robinson tries to persuade his mother to talk to his father. 3 The storm takes place. 5 The ship leaves the River Humber. 4 Robinson's father advises him not to go to sea. 2	1
9	**Award 2 marks** for any two reasonable inferences. For example: • It was easier to pronounce than their original name/Kreutznaer. • It sounded more like an English name. • It helped them to fit in to their new surroundings. **Award 1 mark** for any one of the above.	2
10	**Award 1 mark** for: What became of my second brother I never knew, any more than my father or mother knew what became of me.	1
11	**Award 2 marks** for answers that explain both of the following: • He says that the father gave *commands*. • The mother tries to persuade (*persuasions*). **Award 1 mark** for either of the above.	2
12	**Award 2 marks** for any two of: • His father had already given his answer. • He was scared of his father. • His mother was less against the idea. • He thought his mother was more likely to succeed. **Award 1 mark** for any of the above.	2
13	**Award 2 marks** for reasonable answers that include an explanation. Possible responses include: • It will survive, because Robinson is still alive. • It will survive, because he says he saw bigger waves a few days later. • It will sink, because the waves are so high. **Award 1 mark** for reasonable answers that do not include an explanation.	2
14	**Award 3 marks** for any three of: • The ship gets into trouble almost as soon as it sets sail. • Robinson was sick in mind and body. • Robinson does not think he will survive the storm. • Robinson has an *agony of mind*. • Robinson says he will go back to his father and take his advice because of his miseries. **Award 2 marks** for any two of the above. **Award 1 mark** for any of the above.	3
15	**Award 2 marks** for: • I expected every wave would have swallowed us up • we should never rise more. **Award 1 mark** for either of the above.	2
16	**Award 2 marks** for: • At first he wanted to ignore all of his father's advice or he thought his father was wrong. • At the end he realises that his father was right. **Award 1 mark** for either of the above.	2

Answer grids

Answer grids

Focus: Words in context

Test	Text	Question number	Actual marks	Possible marks	Workbooks links
1	Oscar to the Rescue	1, 2, 3		3	
2	Icarus and Daedalus	1, 2, 3		3	
3	The Charge of the Light Brigade	1, 2, 3		3	
4	Wheelchair Warrior	1, 2, 3		3	page 6–11, page 66–73 (general practice)
5	Skiathos	1, 2, 3		3	
6	The Diary of Samuel Pepys	1, 2, 3		3	
7	Hard Times	1, 2, 3		3	
8	Brazil	1, 2, 3		3	
9	Robinson Crusoe	1, 2, 3		3	
Total across all tests				27	

Focus: Retrieval/identification

Test	Text	Question number	Actual marks	Possible marks	Workbooks links
1	Oscar to the Rescue	4, 5, 6		3	
2	Icarus and Daedalus	4, 5, 6		3	
3	The Charge of the Light Brigade	4, 5, 6		3	
4	Wheelchair Warrior	4, 5, 6		4	page 12–28, page 66–73 (general practice)
5	Skiathos	4, 5, 6		4	
6	The Diary of Samuel Pepys	4, 5, 6		3	
7	Hard Times	4, 5, 6, 7, 8, 9, 10		7	
8	Brazil	4, 5, 6		3	
9	Robinson Crusoe	4, 5, 6, 7		4	
Total across all tests				34	

Focus: Summarising main ideas

Test	Text	Question number	Actual marks	Possible marks	Workbooks links
1	Oscar to the Rescue	7		3	
2	Icarus and Daedalus	7		3	
3	The Charge of the Light Brigade	7		1	
4	Wheelchair Warrior	7		2	page 29–30, page 66–73 (general practice)
5	Skiathos	7		1	
6	The Diary of Samuel Pepys	7		1	
7	Hard Times	11		1	
8	Brazil	7		1	
9	Robinson Crusoe	8		1	
Total across all tests				14	

Answer grids

Focus: Inference

Test	Text	Question number	Actual marks	Possible marks	Workbooks links
1	Oscar to the Rescue	8, 9, 10, 11, 12		8	
2	Icarus and Daedalus	8, 9, 10, 11, 12, 13		11	
3	The Charge of the Light Brigade	8, 9, 10, 11, 12, 13		8	
4	Wheelchair Warrior	8, 9, 10, 11, 12, 13		10	page 31–47, page 66–73 (general practice)
5	Skiathos	8, 9, 10, 11, 12, 13		8	
6	The Diary of Samuel Pepys	8, 9, 10, 11, 12, 13		8	
7	Hard Times	12, 13, 14, 15		9	
8	Brazil	8, 9, 10, 11, 12, 13		11	
9	Robinson Crusoe	9, 10, 11, 12		7	
Total across all tests				80	

Focus: Prediction

Test	Text	Question number	Actual marks	Possible marks	Workbooks links
1	Oscar to the Rescue	13		2	
2	Icarus and Daedalus	14		1	
3	The Charge of the Light Brigade	14		1	
4	Wheelchair Warrior	14		1	page 48–50, page 66–73 (general practice)
5	Skiathos	14		2	
6	The Diary of Samuel Pepys	14		1	
7	Hard Times	16		2	
8	Brazil	14		2	
9	Robinson Crusoe	13		2	
Total across all tests				14	

Focus: How information is related

Test	Text	Question number	Actual marks	Possible marks	Workbooks links
1	Oscar to the Rescue	14		1	
2	Icarus and Daedalus	15		2	
3	The Charge of the Light Brigade	15		1	
4	Wheelchair Warrior	15		3	page 51–52, page 66–73 (general practice)
5	Skiathos	15		3	
6	The Diary of Samuel Pepys	15		1	
7	Hard Times	17		1	
8	Brazil	15		1	
9	Robinson Crusoe	14		3	
Total across all tests				16	

Answer grids

Focus: How meaning is enhanced

Test	Text	Question number	Actual marks	Possible marks	Workbooks links
1	Oscar to the Rescue	15		2	
2	Icarus and Daedalus	16		1	
3	The Charge of the Light Brigade	16		2	
4	Wheelchair Warrior	16, 17		4	page 53–59, page 66–73 (general practice)
5	Skiathos	16		2	
6	The Diary of Samuel Pepys	16		1	
7	Hard Times	18		2	
8	Brazil	16		1	
9	Robinson Crusoe	15		2	
Total across all tests				17	

Focus: Making comparisons

Test	Text	Question number	Actual marks	Possible marks	Workbooks links
1	Oscar to the Rescue	16		2	
2	Icarus and Daedalus	17		2	
3	The Charge of the Light Brigade	17		2	
4	Wheelchair Warrior	18		2	page 60–62, page 66–73 (general practice)
5	Skiathos	17		3	
6	The Diary of Samuel Pepys	17		2	
7	Hard Times	19		2	
8	Brazil	17		3	
9	Robinson Crusoe	16		2	
Total across all tests				20	